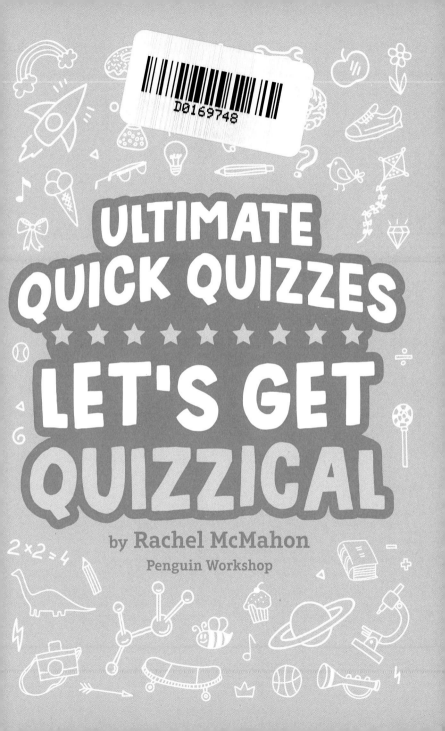

ULTIMATE QUICK QUIZZES

★ ★ ★ ★ ★ ★ ★ ★ ★ ★ ★

LET'S GET QUIZZICAL

by **Rachel McMahon**

Penguin Workshop

D0169748

**For my parents, Brenda and Jeff,
who always have been so supportive of me,
no matter what.**

PENGUIN WORKSHOP
An Imprint of Penguin Random House LLC, New York

Penguin supports copyright. Copyright fuels creativity, encourages diverse voices, promotes free speech, and creates a vibrant culture. Thank you for buying an authorized edition of this book and for complying with copyright laws by not reproducing, scanning, or distributing any part of it in any form without permission. You are supporting writers and allowing Penguin to continue to publish books for every reader.

Photo credits: cover (background): anuwat meereewee/iStock/Getty Images; cover and interior (used throughout): (animals) Bubert/iStock/Getty Images, (books) Natasha_Pankina/iStock/ Getty Images, (breakfast) jamtoons/iStock/Getty Images, (casino) kostenkodesign/iStock/ Getty Images, (children's doodles) saenal78/iStock/Getty Images, (Christmas, Halloween, pastries and bread) Baksiabat/iStock/Getty Images, (dogs) kimberrywood/DigitalVision Vectors/ Getty Images, (fast food) LokFung/DigitalVision Vectors/Getty Images, (fast food, fruits) fleaz/ iStock/Getty Images, (food) topform84/iStock/Getty Images, (Great Dane) feirin/iStock/ Getty Images, (hobbies) Olya Haifisch/iStock/Getty Images, (kawaii animals) tulpahn/iStock/ Getty Images, (kids' animal drawings) zsooofija/iStock/Getty Images, (kids' doodles) sapto7/iStock/ Getty Images, (math and science) Natalie_/iStock/Getty Images, (music) dapoomll/iStock/ Getty Images, (playground) mocoo/iStock/Getty Images, (school) undrey/iStock/Getty Images, (smiley icons) lilipom/iStock/Getty Images, (space) Valeriia Myroshnichenko/iStock/Getty Images, (sports) neapneap/iStock/Getty Images, (summer) Anastasiia Kurman/iStock/Getty Images, (travel) teddybearpicnic/iStock/Getty Images, (TV and movies) Sashatigar/iStock/Getty Images, (underwater life) Tatsiana Zayats/iStock/Getty Images

Visit us online at www.penguinrandomhouse.com.

ISBN 9780593225639   10 9 8 7 6 5 4 3 TC

LET'S GET QUIZZICAL

★ ★ ★ ★ ★

No need to stress or worry, these aren't your average quizzes! You are for sure going to get an A+ on them.

Get quizzical and learn more about who you are as a person, with a back-to-school theme. These quizzes turn simple things like school subjects, school supplies, and everyday school activities into something you've never experienced before. Get ready to learn about the most important student . . . YOU!

WE'LL GUESS YOUR FAVORITE SCHOOL SUBJECT BASED ON YOUR FAVORITE THINGS

1. **Which is your favorite sea creature?**
   a. Jellyfish
   b. Dolphin
   c. Sea turtle
   d. Starfish
   e. Shark
   f. Whale

2. **Which is your favorite color?**
   a. Red
   b. Orange
   c. Yellow
   d. Green
   e. Blue
   f. Purple

3. **Which is your favorite candy?**
   a. Candy canes
   b. Gummy bears
   c. Candy corn
   d. Chocolate bars
   e. Sour gummy worms
   f. Jelly beans

4. **Which is your favorite breakfast food?**
   a. Cereal
   b. French toast
   c. Waffles
   d. Pancakes
   e. Oatmeal
   f. Cinnamon rolls

5. Which is your favorite holiday?
   a. New Year's
   b. Halloween
   c. Fourth of July
   d. Easter
   e. Thanksgiving
   f. Christmas

6. Which is your favorite game?
   a. Hide-and-Seek
   b. Simon Says
   c. Four Square
   d. Hopscotch
   e. Dodgeball
   f. Freeze Tag

7. Which is your favorite cheesy food?
   a. Grilled cheese sandwich
   b. Pizza
   c. Cheese fries
   d. Macaroni and cheese
   e. Nachos
   f. Quesadilla

8. Which is your favorite sport?
   a. Baseball
   b. Basketball
   c. Soccer
   d. Gymnastics
   e. Football
   f. Volleyball

9. Which is your favorite type of cookie?
   a. Sugar cookie
   b. Peanut butter cookie
   c. Butter cookie
   d. Chocolate chip cookie
   e. Oreos
   f. Snickerdoodle cookie

10. Which is your favorite farm animal?
    a. Sheep
    b. Goat
    c. Cow
    d. Horse
    e. Pig
    f. Rooster

★ ★ ★ ★ ★ ★ ★ ★ ★

If you chose mostly A's—You got **MATH**

If you chose mostly B's—You got **SCIENCE**

If you chose mostly C's—You got **HISTORY**

If you chose mostly D's—You got **ENGLISH**

If you chose mostly E's—You got **GYM**

If you chose mostly F's—You got **MUSIC**

★ ★ ★ ★ ★ ★ ★ ★ ★

CHOOSE SOME SCHOOL SUBJECTS AND WE'LL GUESS IF YOU PREFER CATS OR DOGS

1. Choose one:
   a. Science
   b. Language arts

2. Choose one:
   a. Computers
   b. Reading

3. Choose one:
   a. Math
   b. Writing

4. Choose one:
   a. Gym
   b. Music

5. Choose one:
   a. Social studies
   b. Foreign language

6. Choose one:
   a. Painting
   b. Dance

7. Choose one:
   a. Science
   b. Math

8. Choose one:
   a. Music
   b. Art

9. Choose one:
   a. Social studies
   b. Science

10. Choose one:
    a. Lunch
    b. Recess

If you chose mostly A's—You got **DOGS**

If you chose mostly B's—You got **CATS**

WHICH TYPE OF BOOK ARE YOU?

1. Which of these would you want as a pet?
   a. Cat
   b. Dog
   c. Hamster
   d. Fish

2. Which of these foods would you eat for lunch?
   a. Macaroni and cheese
   b. Chicken nuggets
   c. Peanut butter and jelly sandwich
   d. Buttered noodles

3. Which season is your favorite?
   a. Fall
   b. Winter
   c. Spring
   d. Summer

4. Which superpower would you want?
   a. Super strength
   b. Super speed
   c. Invisibility
   d. The ability to fly

5. Which ice cream flavor is the best?
   a. Strawberry
   b. Rocky road
   c. Vanilla
   d. Chocolate

6. Which dessert is the best?
   a. Cupcakes
   b. Ice cream
   c. Pie
   d. Brownies

7. Which school subject is the best?
   a. Language arts
   b. History
   c. Math
   d. Science

8. Which snack is your favorite?
   a. Popcorn
   b. Chips
   c. Yogurt
   d. Cookies

9. Which drink is your favorite?
   a. Kool-Aid
   b. Slushy
   c. Lemonade
   d. Soda

10. Where would you want to go on vacation?
    a. Big city
    b. National park
    c. Beach resort
    d. Cruise

11. Choose something to read:
    a. Comic book
    b. Menu
    c. Magazine
    d. Picture book

★ ★ ★ ★ ★ ★ ★ ★ ★ ★

If you chose mostly A's—You got **FICTION BOOKS**

If you chose mostly B's—You got **NONFICTION BOOKS**

If you chose mostly C's—You got **SHORT STORY BOOKS**

If you chose mostly D's—You got **PICTURE BOOKS**

PICK SOME AFTER-SCHOOL SNACKS TO REVEAL WHAT DOG BREED YOU ARE

1. Pick an after-school snack:
   a. Nacho cheese chips
   b. Pudding
   c. Peanuts
   d. Pretzels

2. Pick an after-school snack:
   a. Cheddar cheese chips
   b. Jell-O
   c. Cereal treats
   d. Popcorn

3. Pick an after-school snack:
   a. Potato chips
   b. Apple and peanut butter
   c. Chocolate milk
   d. Cheese and crackers

4. Pick an after-school snack:
   a. Graham crackers
   b. Nachos
   c. Chocolate bar
   d. Goldfish crackers

5. Pick an after-school snack:
   a. Barbeque potato chips
   b. Peanut butter cracker sandwiches
   c. Pudding cup
   d. Party mix

6. Pick an after-school snack:
   a. Cheese popcorn   c. Watermelon
   b. Yogurt   d. Almonds

7. Pick an after-school snack:
   a. Chocolate sandwich cookies
   b. Beef jerky
   c. Cheese stick
   d. Banana

8. Pick an after-school snack:
   a. Pizza rolls   c. Granola bar
   b. Apple   d. Brownie

9. Pick an after-school snack:
   a. Toaster pastries
   b. Sugar cookie
   c. Blueberries
   d. Cinnamon sugar cereal

10. Pick an after-school snack:
    a. Frosted animal crackers   c. Grapes
    b. Chocolate chip muffin   d. Fruity candy

11. Pick an after-school snack:
    a. Doughnut   c. Jelly beans
    b. Carrots   d. Smoothie

12. **Pick an after-school snack:**
    a. Animal crackers
    b. Tortilla chips
    c. Chocolate and peanut butter cereal puffs
    d. Caramel popcorn

13. **Pick an after-school snack:**
    a. Honey graham snacks
    b. Fruit snacks
    c. Whole grain crackers
    d. Peanut butter sandwich cookies

If you chose mostly A's—You got **PUG**

If you chose mostly B's—You got **GREAT DANE**

If you chose mostly C's—You got **POODLE**

If you chose mostly D's—You got **GOLDEN RETRIEVER**

PICK SOME BREAKFAST FOODS AND WE'LL GUESS IF YOU'RE TALKATIVE OR QUIET IN SCHOOL

1. Waffles or pancakes?
   a. Waffles
   b. Pancakes

2. Blueberry pancakes or chocolate chip pancakes?
   a. Blueberry pancakes
   b. Chocolate chip pancakes

3. Cereal or bacon?
   a. Cereal
   b. Bacon

4. Scrambled eggs or sausage?
   a. Scrambled eggs
   b. Sausage

5. Bagel or muffin?
   a. Bagel
   b. Muffin

6. Toast or hash browns?
   a. Toast
   b. Hash browns

7. Cinnamon rolls or doughnuts?
    a. Cinnamon rolls
    b. Doughnuts

8. Chocolate doughnuts or glazed doughnuts?
    a. Chocolate doughnuts
    b. Glazed doughnuts

9. Smoothie or toaster pastries?
    a. Smoothie
    b. Toaster pastries

10. Yogurt or strudel pastries?
    a. Yogurt
    b. Strudel pastries

11. Oatmeal or frozen waffles?
    a. Oatmeal
    b. Frozen waffles

★ ★ ★ ★ ★ ★ ★ ★ ★ ★

If you chose mostly A's—You got **QUIET**

If you chose mostly B's—You got **TALKATIVE**

★ ★ ★ ★ ★ ★ ★ ★ ★ ★

GO BACK-TO-SCHOOL SHOPPING AND WE'LL REVEAL WHICH DESSERT YOU ARE

1. **Choose something to write with:**
   a. Glitter pen
   b. Pencil
   c. Mechanical pencil
   d. Regular pen

2. **What color pencil case do you want?**
   a. Sparkles
   b. Clear
   c. Pink
   d. Blue

3. **What do you want on your backpack?**
   a. Flowers
   b. Stripes
   c. Polka dots
   d. Stars

4. **What color backpack do you want?**
   a. Pink
   b. Black
   c. Blue
   d. A different color

5. **Choose something to draw with:**
   a. Crayons
   b. Colored pencils
   c. Pens
   d. Sharpies

6. **What do you want on your notebook?**
   a. Unicorns
   b. Spaceships
   c. Dogs
   d. Emoji

7. Choose a colored folder:
   a. Purple
   b. Yellow
   c. Red
   d. Green

8. Choose a highlighter color:
   a. Pink
   b. Yellow
   c. Blue
   d. Orange

9. Choose something to decorate your locker with:
   a. Mirror
   b. Whiteboard
   c. Rug
   d. Magnets

10. Choose one more school supply:
   a. Food-shaped erasers
   b. Pencil sharpener
   c. Sticky notes
   d. Binder

If you chose mostly A's—You got **CUPCAKE**

If you chose mostly B's—You got **CHEESECAKE**

If you chose mostly C's—You got **ICE CREAM**

If you chose mostly D's—You got **COOKIE**

WHAT DO YOUR TEACHERS THINK ABOUT YOU?

1. Do you like going to school?
   a. Yes
   b. No
   c. Sometimes

2. Which school subject is your favorite?
   a. Math
   b. Science
   c. English

3. Which school subject is your least favorite?
   a. English
   b. Math
   c. Science

4. What is your favorite thing about school?
   a. Learning cool things
   b. Gym class
   c. Being with friends

5. What is your least favorite thing about school?
   a. Bullies
   b. Homework
   c. Tests

6. Do you bring your own lunch to school or get a hot lunch?
   a. Bring my own lunch
   b. Hot lunch
   c. Both

7. **What is your favorite thing to write with in class?**
   a. Pen
   b. Mechanical pencil
   c. Regular pencil

8. **What is the best thing to do at recess?**
   a. Play a game
   b. Talk with friends
   c. Run around

9. **What is a gift you'd get for your teacher?**
   a. Mug
   b. Their favorite candy
   c. Handmade piece of art

10. **What word best describes you?**
    a. Smart
    b. Cool
    c. Kind

★ ★ ★ ★ ★ ★ ★ ★ ★ ★

If you chose mostly A's—You got **HARDWORKING**

If you chose mostly B's—You got **AWESOME**

If you chose mostly C's—You got **NICE**

★ ★ ★ ★ ★ ★ ★ ★ ★ ★

WHAT KIND OF STUDENT ARE YOU?

1. What time do you wake up in the morning?
   a. 6 a.m. or earlier
   c. 8 a.m. or later
   b. 7 a.m.

2. What do you like to eat for breakfast?
   a. Cereal
   c. Waffles
   b. Pancakes

3. How many best friends do you have?
   a. 1
   c. 4 or more
   b. 2–3

4. What do you like to eat for lunch?
   a. Sandwich
   c. Noodles
   b. Pizza

5. What are you best at?
   a. Music
   c. Art
   b. Sports

6. Which school superpower would you want?
   a. Ability to remember everything you read
   b. Ability to control adults
   c. Ability to write with your finger

7. If you were a teacher, what class would you want to teach?
    a. Science　　　　　　c. Art
    b. History

8. Choose a club to join:
    a. Robot club　　　　　c. Music club
    b. Gaming club

9. Which job would you want in the future?
    a. Astronaut　　　　　c. Dancer
    b. President

10. What is something you are good at?
    a. Getting good grades
    b. Turning work in on time
    c. Raising your hand in class

11. Choose a fun way to get to school:
    a. Bike　　　　　　　　c. Scooter
    b. Hoverboard

★ ★ ★ ★ ★ ★ ★ ★ ★ ★

If you chose mostly A's—You got **SMART**

If you chose mostly B's—You got **NATURAL LEADER**

If you chose mostly C's—You got **ARTIST**

WHICH ANIMAL WOULD BE YOUR IDEAL TEACHER?

1. What makes you happy?
   a. Drawing
   b. Playing games
   c. Eating fast food
   d. Swimming

2. Which is the worst?
   a. Arguing with friends
   b. Going to the doctor
   c. When grown-ups embarrass you
   d. Being grounded

3. Which scares you the most?
   a. Heights
   b. The dark
   c. Snakes
   d. Spiders

4. Who in your family are you closest with?
   a. Pet
   b. Sibling
   c. Dad
   d. Mom

5. What summer activity sounds best?
   a. Going to the zoo
   b. Going to the beach
   c. Having a water balloon fight
   d. Doing a scavenger hunt

6. What winter activity sounds best?
   a. Building a snowman
   b. Sledding
   c. Having a snowball fight
   d. Baking cookies

7. What type of YouTube channel would you want to start?
   a. DIYs
   b. Vlogs
   c. Pranks
   d. Gaming

8. What is your best friend like?
   a. Friendly
   b. Funny
   c. Wild
   d. Awesome

9. Choose a place to spend the day with your friends:
   a. Aquarium
   b. Carnival
   c. Arcade
   d. Zoo

10. Choose a fun job to have:
    a. Cartoon voice-over
    b. YouTube star
    c. Roller coaster tester
    d. Toy designer

11. Which meal is your favorite?
    a. Breakfast
    b. Lunch
    c. Dinner
    d. Dessert

★ ★ ★ ★ ★ ★ ★ ★ ★

If you chose mostly A's—
Your ideal teacher would be an ELEPHANT
This is because you are a big dreamer and someone who seeks harmony, like an elephant.

If you chose mostly B's—
Your ideal teacher would be a DOG
This is because you are someone who is energetic and the life of the party, like a dog.

If you chose mostly C's—
Your ideal teacher would be a GRIZZLY BEAR
This is because you are someone who can be fierce and confident, like a grizzly bear.

If you chose mostly D's—
Your ideal teacher would be a TIGER
This is because you are someone who is intelligent and strong, like a tiger.

★ ★ ★ ★ ★ ★ ★ ★ ★

WHAT SUBJECT ARE YOU?

1. If you were to start a charity, what would you raise money for?
   - a. Disaster relief
   - b. Animals
   - c. Affordable housing
   - d. Sick children

2. What kind of fundraiser is your favorite?
   - a. Walkathon
   - b. Art show
   - c. Talent show
   - d. Selling candy

3. What is the best playground equipment?
   - a. Sports fields/courts
   - b. Slides
   - c. Monkey bars
   - d. Swings

4. Where would you most want to go swimming?
   - a. Beach
   - b. Lake
   - c. Water park
   - d. Pool

5. Which animal are you most like?
   - a. Dog
   - b. Cat
   - c. Bird
   - d. Fish

6. What annoys you the most?
   a. When people interrupt others when they're talking
   b. Being ignored by others
   c. No Wi-Fi
   d. Invasion of your personal space

7. Which would be the best present to receive?
   a. Journal   c. Slime
   b. Gel pens   d. Book

8. Which weird food combination would you most likely try?
   a. Ketchup on popcorn   c. Hot dog with jelly
   b. Spaghetti tacos   d. Cheetos and milk

9. Which season is your favorite?
   a. Winter   c. Summer
   b. Fall   d. Spring

10. How organized are you?
   a. Very unorganized   c. Somewhat organized
   b. Unorganized   d. Very organized

11. What is your favorite part of the school day?
   a. Leaving at the end of the day
   b. Seeing your friends
   c. Lunch
   d. Your favorite class

★ ★ ★ ★ ★ ★ ★ ★ ★

If you chose mostly A's—You got SOCIAL STUDIES
You are someone who likes to learn about the past and how we can make the future a better one.

If you chose mostly B's—You got ENGLISH
You are someone who likes to express yourself creatively.

If you chose mostly C's—You got SCIENCE
You are someone who likes to experiment with things in the world. You have a curious mind.

If you chose mostly D's—You got MATH
You are someone who is a logical thinker. You are a rule-follower and like to get things done the right way.

★ ★ ★ ★ ★ ★ ★ ★ ★

ARE YOU A PEN OR A PENCIL?

1. **Dogs or cats?**
   a. Dogs   b. Cats

2. **Singing or dancing?**
   a. Singing   b. Dancing

3. **TikTok or YouTube?**

   a. TikTok   b. YouTube

4. **Ice cream or cake?**
   a. Ice cream   b. Cake

5. **Hamburgers or tacos?**
   a. Hamburgers   b. Tacos

6. **Phone or TV?**
   a. Phone   b. TV

7. **Sour or sweet candy?**
   a. Sour candy   b. Sweet candy

8. **Plane or train?**

   a. Plane   b. Train

9. **Veggies or fruits?**
   a. Veggies b. Fruits

10. **Sports or art?**
    a. Sports b. Art

11. **Winter or summer?**
    a. Winter b. Summer

12. **Slushies or Popsicles?**
    a. Slushies b. Popsicles

13. **Night or morning?**
    a. Night b. Morning

★ ★ ★ ★ ★ ★ ★ ★ ★ ★

If you chose mostly A's—You got PEN
You're someone who is outgoing and daring.
You aren't scared of much.

If you chose mostly B's—You got PENCIL
You're someone who is creative and kind.
You have big dreams.

★ ★ ★ ★ ★ ★ ★ ★ ★ ★

CHOOSE SOME ANIMALS TO FIND OUT WHICH CATEGORY OF BOOK YOU ARE

1. Choose an animal:
   a. Chimpanzee
   b. Hippopotamus
   c. Hyena
   d. Ostrich

2. Choose an animal:
   a. Dolphin
   b. Crocodile
   c. Flamingo
   d. Whale

3. Choose an animal:
   a. Dog
   b. Eagle
   c. Seahorse
   d. Kangaroo

4. Choose an animal:
   a. Elephant
   b. Gorilla
   c. Giraffe
   d. Wolf

5. Choose an animal:
   a. Rat
   b. Jaguar
   c. Zebra
   d. Sloth

6. Choose an animal:
   a. Parrot
   b. Shark
   c. Sea turtle
   d. Ferret

7. Choose an animal:
   a. Octopus
   b. Rhinoceros
   c. Alpaca
   d. Hamster

8. Choose an animal:
   a. Sea lion
   b. Panther
   c. Squirrel
   d. Owl

9. Choose an animal:
   a. Goat
   b. Raccoon
   c. Duck
   d. Mouse

10. Choose an animal:
    a. Horse
    b. Cheetah
    c. Goose
    d. Cat

11. Choose an animal:
    a. Orangutan
    b. Polar bear
    c. Llama
    d. Tortoise

12. Choose an animal:
    a. Jellyfish
    b. Fox
    c. Penguin
    d. Koala bear

13. **Choose an animal:**
    a. Pig
    c. Snake
    b. Tiger
    d. Deer

14. **Choose an animal:**
    a. Sheep
    c. Camel
    b. Lion
    d. Rabbit

15. **Choose an animal:**
    a. Skunk
    c. Donkey
    b. Porcupine
    d. Chicken

If you chose mostly A's—You got **NONFICTION**
You're someone who is smart and honest.

If you chose mostly B's—You got **MYSTERY**
You're someone who is daring and bold.

If you chose mostly C's—You got **FICTION**
You're someone who is wild and unique.

If you chose mostly D's—You got **POETRY**
You're someone who is loving and dramatic.

WHICH FUNNY-NAMED CRAYON ARE YOU?

1. Which type of music is your favorite?
    a. Pop
    b. Country
    c. Rock
    d. Rap
    e. Show tunes

2. Which type of movie is your favorite?
    a. Comedy
    b. Animated
    c. Action
    d. Science fiction
    e. Family-friendly

3. What cake flavor do you like best?
    a. Funfetti
    b. Chocolate
    c. Red velvet
    d. Lemon
    e. Vanilla

4. Which is the best way to get around?
    a. Scooter
    b. Bike
    c. Skateboard
    d. Hoverboard
    e. Rollerblades

5. Which food is your favorite?
    a. Macaroni and cheese
    b. Ice cream
    c. Spaghetti
    d. Chicken nuggets
    e. Pizza

6. **What fruit is your favorite?**
   a. Bananas
   b. Apples
   c. Strawberries
   d. Grapes
   e. Watermelon

7. **What is something you are good at?**
   a. Making people laugh
   b. Making people smile
   c. Trying scary things
   d. Storytelling
   e. Giving hugs

8. **What is your favorite thing to get at the movie theater?**
   a. Soft pretzel
   b. Chocolate candy
   c. Slushy
   d. Popcorn
   e. Fruity candy

9. **What is your favorite thing to do at a park?**
   a. Play games
   b. Have a picnic
   c. Look for wildlife
   d. Hunt for bugs
   e. Go on the playground

10. **Which dog breed is the best?**
    a. Pug
    b. Poodle
    c. Chihuahua
    d. Dalmatian
    e. Golden retriever

★ ★ ★ ★ ★ ★ ★ ★ ★ ★

If you chose mostly A's—You got MACARONI AND CHEESE
You're wacky and funny.

If you chose mostly B's—You got TICKLE ME PINK
You're nice and sweet.

If you chose mostly C's—You got RAZZMATAZZ
You're outgoing and spontaneous.

If you chose mostly D's—You got INCHWORM
You're unique and bold.

If you chose mostly E's—You got FUZZY WUZZY
You're friendly and loving.

★ ★ ★ ★ ★ ★ ★ ★ ★ ★

WHAT LUNCH SHOULD YOU BRING TO SCHOOL?

1. Choose a stack of pancakes:
   a. Blueberry pancakes
   b. Chocolate chip pancakes
   c. Regular pancakes

2. Choose a flavor of popcorn:
   a. Caramel popcorn
   b. Cheese popcorn
   c. Buttered popcorn

3. Choose a fruit:
   a. Strawberries
   b. Watermelon
   c. Apples

4. Choose a vegetable:
   a. Carrots
   b. Corn
   c. Celery

5. Choose a flavor of chips:
   a. Sour cream and onion
   b. Cheddar
   c. Barbeque

6. Choose a pizza topping:
   a. Pepperoni
   b. Cheese
   c. Ham

7. Choose a doughnut:
   a. Powdered
   b. Cinnamon sugar
   c. Glazed

8. Choose some crackers:
   a. Ritz cracker sandwiches
   b. Cheez-Its
   c. Goldfish crackers

9. Choose a pastry:
   a. Muffins
   b. Cinnamon rolls
   c. Doughnut holes

10. Choose some pasta:
    a. Spaghetti
    b. Ravioli
    c. Lasagna

11. Choose a cheesy food:
    a. Grilled cheese sandwich
    b. Pizza
    c. Cheese quesadilla

12. Choose a sandwich:
    a. Ham and cheese
    b. Cheeseburger
    c. Sloppy joe

13. Choose a drink:
    a. Smoothie
    b. Milkshake
    c. Slushy

⭐ ⭐ ⭐ ⭐ ⭐ ⭐ ⭐ ⭐ ⭐ ⭐

If you chose mostly A's—
You got **PEANUT BUTTER AND JELLY SANDWICH**

If you chose mostly B's—You got **LEFTOVER PIZZA**

If you chose mostly C's—You got **TACOS**

WHAT BIRTHDAY TREAT SHOULD YOU BRING TO SCHOOL?

1. Which food is your favorite?
   a. Burger
   b. Pizza
   c. Tacos

2. Which dessert is your favorite?
   a. Cookies
   b. Brownies
   c. Pie

3. What do you like to do on the weekend?
   a. Play video games
   b. Make crafts
   c. Hang with friends

4. How do you like your ice cream?
   a. In a waffle cone
   b. In a cake cone
   c. In a bowl

5. What is your favorite thing about yourself?
   a. Your brains
   b. Your looks
   c. Your sense of humor

6. Which social media app seems the least fun?
   a. Instagram
   b. Twitter
   c. Snapchat

7. **Which type of frosting is your favorite?**
   a. Cream cheese
   b. Buttercream
   c. Whipped cream

8. **Which doughnut flavor is the worst?**
   a. Jelly-filled
   b. Cream-filled
   c. Blueberry

9. **What time of day is your favorite?**
   a. Night
   b. Afternoon
   c. Morning

10. **Which holiday candy is the best?**
    a. Valentine's Day conversation hearts
    b. Easter jelly beans
    c. Halloween candy corn

11. **What is your favorite thing to write with in school?**
    a. Pencil
    b. Pen
    c. Mechanical pencil

★ ★ ★ ★ ★ ★ ★ ★ ★ ★

If you chose mostly A's—You got **RICE KRISPIES TREATS**

If you chose mostly B's—You got **CUPCAKES**

If you chose mostly C's—You got **DOUGHNUTS**

WHAT CAFETERIA FOOD ARE YOU?

1. Where would you prefer to sit in a classroom?
   a. Near the teacher
   b. In the back
   c. In the middle
   d. In the front

2. What do you like to do most at the beach?
   a. Toss a ball around
   b. Mess around with your friends
   c. Play in the water
   d. Bury people and yourself in the sand

3. Where would be the coolest place to go on a field trip?
   a. Pumpkin patch
   b. Science museum
   c. Roller-skating
   d. Aquarium

4. What's the best thing to put on a sandwich?
   a. Meat
   b. Peanut butter
   c. Cheese
   d. Jelly

5. Which side dish is the tastiest?
   a. French fries
   b. Chips
   c. Tater tots
   d. Onion rings

6. Which style of french fries is your favorite?
   a. Crinkle-cut fries
   b. Skinny-cut fries
   c. Smiley-face fries
   d. Waffle fries

7. What color do you like the most?
   a. Yellow   b. Blue   c. Purple   d. Green

8. What color do you like the least?
   a. Green   b. Yellow   c. Blue   d. Purple

9. How would you like to be famous?
   a. Be in movies
   b. Be the voice of a cartoon character
   c. Be a YouTuber
   d. Be on a kids TV show

10. Which drink is your favorite?
    a. Water   b. Milk   c. Soda   d. Juice

11. Which drink is your least favorite?
    a. Soda   b. Juice   c. Water   d. Milk

★ ★ ★ ★ ★ ★ ★ ★ ★

If you chose mostly A's—You got HAMBURGER
You're chummy.

If you chose mostly B's—You got FISH STICKS
You're sneaky.

If you chose mostly C's—You got SLOPPY JOES
You're wild.

If you chose mostly D's—You got MAC AND CHEESE
You're funny.

WHAT SCHOOL HOLIDAY ARE YOU?

1. Which type of food is your favorite?
   a. American food
   b. Italian food
   c. Chinese food
   d. Mexican food

2. Which compliment would you most like to receive?
   a. You're so fun
   b. You're so cute
   c. You're so smart
   d. You're so kind

3. What party would you like to throw for your friends?
   a. Halloween
   b. Valentine's Day
   c. St. Patrick's Day
   d. Thanksgiving

4. Which flavor combination sounds the tastiest?
   a. Salt and pepper
   b. Chocolate and strawberry
   c. Meat and cheese
   d. Apple and cinnamon

5. What makes you the happiest?
   a. Puppies
   b. Friends
   c. Kittens
   d. Babies

6. You find out your crush likes you back, what do you do?
   a. Wait for them to tell you
   b. Go talk to them
   c. Ask them to date you
   d. Get them a gift

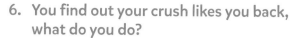

7. Which gym game is the best?
   a. Relay races
   c. Dodgeball
   b. Soccer
   d. Tag

8. What is your favorite thing about the summer?
   a. No school
   c. The food
   b. The weather
   d. Hanging with friends

9. How old would you want to stay forever?
   a. 8 years old
   c. 18 years old
   b. 13 years old
   d. 21 years old

If you chose mostly A's—
You got THE 100TH DAY OF SCHOOL

You are lively, festive, and cheerful. You like to have fun and are willing to celebrate any possible occasion.

If you chose mostly B's—You got VALENTINE'S DAY

You are affectionate and bold. You are someone who is not afraid to show their emotions.

If you chose mostly C's—
You got NATIONAL YOUNG READERS DAY

You are someone with a brilliant mind. You love to challenge yourself so you can become the best person you can possibly be.

If you chose mostly D's—You got EARTH DAY

You care deeply about the people and world around you. You have a big heart and are always willing to share it with others.

WHAT COLOR LUNCH BOX SHOULD YOU HAVE?

1. Which color combination is your favorite?
   a. Red and blue
   b. Blue and green
   c. Yellow and pink
   d. Pink and purple
   e. Black and white

2. Which color is your least favorite?
   a. Yellow
   b. Pink
   c. Black
   d. Blue
   e. Red

3. Which pattern is your favorite?
   a. Plaid
   b. Vertical stripes
   c. Polka dots
   d. Zebra print
   e. Horizontal stripes

4. Which pattern is your least favorite?
   a. Polka dots
   b. Zebra print
   c. Horizontal stripes
   d. Plaid
   e. Vertical stripes

5. If you had to change your name to a color, which would you pick?
   a. Magenta   d. Fuchsia
   b. Ocean   e. Ebony
   c. Daffodil

6. What color would you like to paint your room?
   a. Maroon   d. Purple
   b. Grey   e. Dark blue
   c. Peach

7. What color do you associate with happiness?
   a. Red   d. Pink
   b. Bright blue e. Orange
   c. Yellow

8. What color do you associate with anger?
   a. Dark red   d. Dark yellow
   b. Orange   e. Black
   c. Bright red

9. What color do you associate with sadness?
   a. Dark blue   d. White
   b. Light blue   e. Black
   c. Grey

10. Choose a black-and-white animal:
- a. Skunk
- b. Cow
- c. Penguin
- d. Zebra
- e. White tiger

11. Choose a red food:
- a. Tomatoes
- b. Cherries
- c. Apples
- d. Strawberries
- e. Red peppers

★ ★ ★ ★ ★ ★ ★ ★ ★

If you chose mostly A's—You got **RED**

If you chose mostly B's—You got **BLUE**

If you chose mostly C's—You got **YELLOW**

If you chose mostly D's—You got **PINK**

If you chose mostly E's—You got **BLACK**

★ ★ ★ ★ ★ ★ ★ ★ ★

WHAT COLOR HIGHLIGHTER ARE YOU?

1. Which accessory is the best?
   a. Bracelet
   b. Earrings
   c. Necklace
   d. Sunglasses
   e. Hat

2. Which sweet food is the best?
   a. Ice cream
   b. Cake
   c. Brownies
   d. Cookies
   e. Pie

3. Which salty food is the best?
   a. Almonds
   b. Pretzels
   c. Cashews
   d. Chips
   e. Peanuts

4. Which sport is the best?
   a. Basketball
   b. Soccer
   c. Volleyball
   d. Football
   e. Baseball

5. Which type of movie is the best?
   a. Action
   b. Adventure
   c. Romance
   d. Comedy
   e. Horror

6. Which school subject is the best?
   a. Science
   b. Math
   c. English
   d. Gym
   e. History

7. Which writing utensil is the best?
   a. Glitter pens
   b. Pencils
   c. Colored pens
   d. Black pens
   e. Mechanical pencils

8. Which meal is the best?
   a. Breakfast
   b. Lunch
   c. Dinner
   d. Dessert
   e. Snacks

9. What time of day is the best?
   a. Morning
   b. Early afternoon
   c. Late afternoon
   d. Evening
   e. Night

10. Which type of book is the best?
    a. Science fiction
    b. Fiction
    c. Mystery
    d. Horror
    e. Fairy tale

11. Which fruit is the best?

a. Blueberries
b. Apples
c. Strawberries
d. Bananas
e. Watermelon

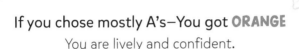

★ ★ ★ ★ ★ ★ ★ ★ ★ ★

If you chose mostly A's—You got ORANGE
You are lively and confident.

If you chose mostly B's—You got YELLOW
You are a content and kindhearted person.

If you chose mostly C's—You got PINK
You are mature and deeply value your relationships
with your loved ones.

If you chose mostly D's—You got GREEN
You are immature at times, but people know they
can always turn to you for a good time.

If you chose mostly E's—You got BLUE
You are a strong-willed and entertaining person.

★ ★ ★ ★ ★ ★ ★ ★ ★ ★

WE CAN GUESS IF YOU HAVE A HOT LUNCH OR A COLD LUNCH AT SCHOOL

1. Potato chips or french fries?
   a. Potato chips
   b. French fries

2. Slushies or smoothies?
   a. Slushies
   b. Smoothies

3. Country or pop music?
   a. Country music
   b. Pop music

4. Ice cream or cake?
   a. Ice cream
   b. Cake

5. Art or gym?
   a. Art
   b. Gym

6. Blue or red?
   a. Blue
   b. Red

7. Ice-skating or roller-skating?
   a. Ice-skating
   b. Roller-skating

8. Winter or summer?
   a. Winter
   b. Summer

9. Fall or spring?
   a. Fall   b. Spring

10. Gum or suckers?
    a. Gum   b. Suckers

11. Snow or rain?
    a. Snow   b. Rain

12. The moon or the sun?
    a. The moon   b. The sun

13. Are you a morning person or a night person?
    a. Morning person   b. Night person

14. Reading or drawing?
    a. Reading   b. Drawing

15. Building snowmen or sandcastles?
    a. Snowmen   b. Sandcastles

★ ★ ★ ★ ★ ★ ★ ★ ★ ★

If you chose mostly A's—You got **COLD LUNCH**

If you chose mostly B's—You got **HOT LUNCH**

★ ★ ★ ★ ★ ★ ★ ★ ★ ★

ARE YOU A SEESAW OR A SWING?

1. Have you had the same friends for a while?
   a. No
   b. Yes

2. Do you like your teachers better this year or last year?
   a. This year
   b. Last year

3. Do you have any handshakes with your friends?
   a. No
   b. Yes

4. Does your family have any holiday traditions?
   a. No
   b. Yes

5. Which part about school do you like more?
   a. Gym
   b. Lunch

6. Do you give out lots of compliments to people?
   a. No
   b. Yes

7. Where would you rather throw a party?
   a. Arcade
   b. Bowling alley

8. Have you ever redecorated your room?
   a. Yes
   b. No

9. Would you rather be able to turn into a cat or dog?
   a. Cat
   b. Dog

10. **Do you eat the same thing for lunch at school practically every day?**
    a. No   b. Yes

11. **Do you currently have a favorite color?**
    a. No, it changes too often b. Yes

12. **Video chat or texting?**
    a. Video chat   b. Texting

13. **Which would you rather eat?**
    a. The crusts of a sandwich b. The crusts of a pizza

14. **Do you like to try new foods?**
    a. Yes   b. No

15. **Do you like meeting new people?**
    a. Yes   b. No

★ ★ ★ ★ ★ ★ ★ ★ ★ ★

If you chose mostly A's—You got SEESAW
You are someone who doesn't like sticking to one thing.
You like to switch things up in life so it's not so boring.

If you chose mostly B's—You got SWING
You are someone who is positive and organized. You like to
stick with routines and what you know, because it makes
you feel comfortable.

WHAT DOES YOUR SCHOOL BESTIE THINK OF YOU?

1. What three words best describe you?
   a. Outgoing, fun, jokester
   b. Playful, weird, easygoing
   c. Friendly, thoughtful, positive
   d. Smart, organized, hardworking

2. Which would be the worst situation?
   a. Getting in trouble at home
   b. Getting in trouble with a friend
   c. Getting in trouble with a teacher
   d. Getting in trouble with a coach

3. What word would you choose to use instead of *happy*?
   a. Merry
   b. Thrilled
   c. Joyful
   d. Cheerful

4. What word would you choose to use instead of *sad*?
   a. Blue
   b. Gloomy
   c. Heartbroken
   d. Upset

5. What superpower would you give your best friend?
   a. The ability to make hand shadow puppets in any shape
   b. The power to jump over anything that is in front of them
   c. The ability to memorize every book they read
   d. The power to know where anyone is at any moment

6. What food combination best describes you and your bestie?
   a. Burger and fries
   b. Peanut butter and jelly
   c. Milk and cookies
   d. Mac and cheese

7. What gift would you get for you and your bestie?
   a. Matching key chains
   b. Best friend necklaces
   c. Best friend bracelets
   d. Photo collage of the both of you

8. How many close friends do you have?
   a. 1
   b. 2–3
   c. 4–5
   d. 6 or more

9. Which kind of game is your favorite to play with your bestie?
   a. Board game
   b. Video game
   c. Card game
   d. Sports game

10. Which color combination is your favorite?
    a. Blue and green
    b. Orange and yellow
    c. Pink and purple
    d. Blue and red

If you chose mostly A's—You got **HILARIOUS**

If you chose mostly B's—You got **SILLY**

If you chose mostly C's—You got **CARING**

If you chose mostly D's—You got **AMAZING**

WHAT CLASSROOM GAME ARE YOU?

1. What is something you're good at?
   a. Staying focused
   b. Thinking quickly
   c. Thinking outside of the box
   d. Storytelling

2. What is something you're bad at?
   a. Storytelling
   b. Thinking outside of the box
   c. Thinking quickly
   d. Staying focused

3. Which apocalypse would you do best in?
   a. Zombie apocalypse
   c. Ape takeover
   b. Robot revolt
   d. Alien invasion

4. Which word best describes you?
   a. Chill
   c. Talkative
   b. Competitive
   d. Popular

5. Which wild animal are you most like?
   a. Zebra
   c. Lion
   b. Cheetah
   d. Giraffe

6. What part of the day is your favorite?
   a. Eating lunch
   b. Getting to school
   c. Doing your after-school activity
   d. Leaving school

7. Which saying do you live by?
    a. Everything happens for a reason
    b. Never give up
    c. Go big or go home
    d. Work hard, play hard

8. Which future job sounds most fun?
    a. Professional dancer   c. TV show actor
    b. YouTuber   d. Movie director

9. When do you like to do your homework?
    a. Right after school   c. Late at night
    b. At the end of class   d. Whenever you have time

10. What do you like most about yourself?
    a. Your hair   c. Your style
    b. Your smile   d. Your eyes

★ ★ ★ ★ ★ ★ ★ ★ ★

If you chose mostly A's—You got BINGO
You're eager and easygoing.

If you chose mostly B's—You got TRIVIA
You're smart, decisive, and logical.

If you chose mostly C's—You got HANGMAN
You're daring, gutsy, and clever.

If you chose mostly D's—You got HEADS UP, SEVEN UP
You're charming and sneaky.

WHAT PLAYGROUND GAME ARE YOU?

1. Which type of movie is your favorite?
   a. Action
   b. Comedy
   c. Sci-fi

2. Which TV-watching snack is the best?
   a. Popcorn
   b. Candy
   c. Chips

3. What is the first thing you do when you wake up?
   a. Start getting ready
   b. Take a shower
   c. Eat breakfast

4. What are you like when you play games?
   a. Competitive
   b. Somewhat competitive
   c. Not very competitive

5. Which type of game show would you want to go on?
   a. Athletic game show
   b. Daring game show
   c. Trivia game show

6. What would you add to your bucket list?
   a. Swim with dolphins
   b. Hot-air balloon ride
   c. Win a big competition

7. Are you more loud or quiet?
   a. Loud
   b. It depends
   c. Quiet

8. Which do you use the most?
   a. Phone
   b. Computer
   c. Television

9. Choose a cheesy food:
   a. Pizza
   b. Cheesy potatoes
   c. Macaroni and cheese

10. Which animal would you pick to be your pet?
    a. Kangaroo
    b. Tiger
    c. Owl

11. Which activity sounds the most fun?
    a. Kickball
    b. Jenga
    c. Ribbon dancing

If you chose mostly A's—You got **TAG**

You are someone who is athletic, energetic, and ambitious.

If you chose mostly B's—You got **THE FLOOR IS LAVA**

You are someone who is gutsy, bold, and exciting.

If you chose mostly C's—You got **JUMP ROPE**

You are someone who is gifted, kind, and talented.

ARE YOU GLITTER OR GLUE BASED ON YOUR FAVORITE ACTIVITIES?

1. Choose an activity:
   a. Water balloon fight
   b. Nerf gun battle

2. Choose an activity:
   a. Collecting stickers
   b. Jump rope

3. Choose an activity:
   a. Puzzles
   b. Reading

4. Choose an activity:
   a. Playing with sidewalk chalk
   b. Shooting hoops

5. Choose an activity:
   a. Playing with slime
   b. Playing with bugs

6. Choose an activity:
   a. Swimming
   b. Jumping off diving boards

7. Choose an activity:
   a. Jumping on a trampoline
   b. Zip-lining

8. Choose an activity:
   a. Doing cartwheels
   b. Rock climbing

9. Choose an activity:
   a. Painting
   b. Rock collecting

10. Choose an activity:
    a. Origami
    b. Card collecting

If you chose mostly A's—You got GLITTER
You are cheerful, bright, and extravagant.

If you chose mostly B's—You got GLUE
You are tough, brave, and awesome.

ARE YOU MATH OR SCIENCE?

1. Puzzles or board games?
   a. Puzzles
   b. Board games

2. Glitter slime or regular slime?
   a. Glitter slime
   b. Regular slime

3. Make cookies or make jewelry?
   a. Make cookies
   b. Make jewelry

4. Peanut butter cookies or sugar cookies?
   a. Peanut butter cookies
   b. Sugar cookies

5. Poop emoji or laughing face emoji?
   a. Poop emoji
   b. Laughing face emoji

6. Roller-skating or bowling?
   a. Roller-skating
   b. Bowling

7. Are you quiet in school?
   a. No
   b. Yes

8. Would you rather be able to play the guitar or the piano?
   a. Guitar
   b. Piano

9. Would you rather learn to read lips or learn sign language?
   a. Read lips
   b. Learn sign language

10. Ride a camel or ride a horse?
    a. Ride a camel
    b. Ride a horse

11. Pizza for breakfast or pancakes for dinner?
    a. Pizza for breakfast
    b. Pancakes for dinner

★ ★ ★ ★ ★ ★ ★ ★ ★

If you chose mostly A's—You got SCIENCE
You are a curious and wild person.

If you chose mostly B's—You got MATH
You are a hardworking and responsible person.